Hoping Against All Hope

Hoping Against All Hope

Helder Camara

Translated by
Matthew J. O'Connell

ORBIS BOOKS
Maryknoll, New York

DOVE COMMUNICATIONS
Melbourne, Australia

GILL AND MACMILLAN
Dublin

"We Can Change Our Lives," "We Can Control Our Tides and Our Moons," "Never to Fall Is Not the Important Thing," "Hope in the Midst of Suffering," "Hope in the Midst of Wretchedness," "Hope in the Face of Persecution," "Hope and the Frustration of Human Dialogue," "Hope and the Madness of th Arms Race," "Hope and the Ideology of National Security," "Hope and th Waste of Raw Materials," "Hope of the Water and the Stones," "Hope and th Multinationals," "Hope of Overcoming Selfishness," "Hope Strengthened b the Universities," "Hope from the Alliance of the Weak with the Weak," an "The Beginning of the Beginning of the Day" were originally written in French b Dom Helder Camara at the explicit request of his friends, Bernhard Moosbrugge and Gladys Weigner, founder-owners of pendo-verlag, 8032 Zurich, whic published these works in a German translation in 1981. This English translatio was prepared from a comparative reading of both the French and the Germa texts.

"Put Your Ear to the Ground," "Hope without Risk," "Go Down," "Hope f Despairing Youth," and "Are the Institutions Hopeless?" were original published in *The Desert Is Fertile* by Dom Helder Camara, © 1974 by Orb Books.

Manuscript Editor: William E. Jerman
Photo Editor: Catherine Costello

Photo Credits:
Fr. Don Bank: p. 56
Jeff Brass: p. 70
Mike Gable: p. 30
Fr. Joseph Hahn: pp. 2, 11, 19
Maryknoll Sisters: p. 8
John Padula: p. 23
UNPA Taipei: p. 68
Joe Vail: pp. 36, 78
Eric Wheater: pp. 45, 74

Library of Congress Cataloging in Publication Data

Camara, Helder, 1909-
  Hoping against all hope.

  Translation of: Hoffer wider alle Hoffnung.
  1. Meditations. I. Title.
BX2184.C2713   1984   242   83-19348
ISBN 0-88344-192-6 (pbk.)

DOVE/ISBN 0-85924-309-5
G&M/ISBN 7171-1338-8

Reflections dedicated to the men and women
    who have lost hope
    or who feel that hope eludes them. . . .

Reflections also dedicated in a spirit of fellowship
    to the men and women
    who with the help of grace
    persevere in hoping against all hope
    and who seek to spread everywhere and to all
    the divine gift of hope.

Contents

Foreword

Since the Second Vatican Council (1962–65) Helder
Camara has been the Latin American bishop most widely
known in Europe. Yet during the four sessions of that assembly of the worldwide Catholic Church he did not address the conciliar fathers even once in the Basilica of St.
Peter. He spoke only in small groups and only about the
major directions of world development. I myself was an
enthusiastic listener as he spoke about the writings of
Teilhard de Chardin, with which he was obviously very
familiar. His remarks always had about them something
visionary, which he managed to link to very concrete
events, thus lending them a surprising but very plausible
transparency. He often passed harsh judgments, but he
never stopped there; for him these were only shadows that
made the light stand out more brightly, passageways
through which one came out into the open. For him everything was in movement toward a better, more human future for the world—a movement taking the form of an
experience of God that was already everywhere palpable.

This bishop from the slums of Rio de Janeiro was no
dreamer. He stood with both feet in the muck and degen-
eracy of the straightjacketed world of the shantytowns.
He sought to help with grandiose plans (and a bit of

money), and he failed. The experience changed his approach, but not his vision of the world. At the council he was a friend of Cardinal Montini (later Pope Paul VI) and a close associate of the progressive Belgian Cardinal Suenens. He played an important role in the "poor church" group, which comprised mainly Latin American bishops but thought in worldwide terms. These bishops, closely united to their people, made their presence felt, without pomp or splendor. They were not imitated around the world, but in Latin America the movement led to the momentous assembly of Latin American bishops at Medellín (1968).

During the council there was already talk of the basic communities, which consisted of groups of lay persons within the gigantic official parishes for which hardly any meaningful pastoral provision could be made. These communities were renewing the church, especially in Brazil. Helder Camara became, from our standpoint in Europe, the herald of ecclesial and social renewal. He came to us—not in order to beg for the poor farmers and fishers of Olinda and Recife, the diocese whose shepherd he has been since 1963, but rather in order to make us aware of social problems that were in fact worldwide, though they had become especially evident in Latin America.

Many Europeans did not fully grasp the situation. They went on pilgrimages to Brazil and studied social and psychological problems for three or four semesters. This was certainly instructive, but it did not get Dom Helder's point across to them. Just as it was certainly wrong to apply European methods (in the pastoral area, for example) as a remedy for Latin America, so too it would be an error to apply Brazilian models of renewal, unaltered, to Europe! Yet both of these courses were tried and are to some extent still being tried today. Even bishops and church organizations have made mistakes in this respect. That was not what Dom Helder wanted: he thinks in worldwide terms and he wants to point out what it is that links the whole world together—both the evils and the promise of the future—because no one stands alone. He is talking about "nets" that are spread, or are to be spread, over the entire world.

This is neither egalitarianism nor reductionism to mass uniformity. Helder Camara is able to point to phenomena that may outwardly seem quite different but in reality are complementary. The *whole* must be known and dealt with, even if perhaps in contrary ways.

Helder Camara is extremely flexible and yet ever the same. One need only read José de Broucker's *The Conversions of a Bishop* (London: Collins, 1979). This book consists of conversations in which Câmara tells the story of his life with all its transformations. Through all the changes the basic Christian direction of his faith does not become blurred but rather becomes ever clearer.

Now that Helder Camara is over seventy years old, there have been other retrospects that are even much more instructive inasmuch as they reveal, as it were, the inner side of his personality. One of them, *Mach aus mir einen Regenbogen* (Make of me a rainbow) (Zurich: pendo-verlag, 1981), contains short, almost poetic reflections that are a record of his nocturnal meditations. For it is his practice to spend an hour in prayer to God every night. Not an easy exercise, but one that gives unity to life amid all the confusion. Anyone who has become accustomed to it will not abandon it.

The other retrospect is the present collection of texts that Helder Camara wrote for his friends in Zurich in connection with the tenth anniversary of pendo-verlag. At the same time the texts commemorate the fiftieth anniversary of his own priesthood. They carry a dedication to all those who have lost hope or whom hope eludes. This reminds us of his efforts over many years to gather and form "Abrahamitic minorities" throughout the world.

The expression "Abrahamitic" (in this book he speaks of "various groups practicing active nonviolence") refers to the tribal ancestor Abraham whose hope against all hope was the characteristic mark of his faith. St. Paul never wearied of impressing this point on Christians. No one who knows the jubilarian can doubt that he is permeated and sustained by this hope. It is this that gives his personality its fascination.

But more must be said: Helder Camara is a realist and insists that this hope against all hope is not a theory but a reality! His own experiences as a pastor prove it to him. For this reason he recounts incidents in his dealings with people whose suffering is hopeless.

In Camara's approach to the sick there is no sanctimoniousness, no artificiality, but only faith that is lived with simplicity and is absolutely sure of itself. These examples are in fact overwhelming in their very simplicity; they convince.

There is still another point: at the beginning of Vatican II, in his encyclical *Peace on Earth* John XXIII spoke emphatically of the signs of developments in our time toward peace and the acknowledgment of human dignity. He was referring to events all over the world, and outside the churches—events that are taking place before our eyes. Helder Camara makes this same thought his own in his addresses.

Most public voices echoing concern tell us *only* of the fear aroused by the arms race, the threat represented by ideologies of violence, the irresponsible waste of raw materials, the sinister and impenetrable power of the multinational corporations, the dangerous struggle between specialized sciences, the sophisticated selfishness of seemingly humanitarian political plans, and so on. They project a worldwide, ever deepening anxiety that, as it were, poisons our atmosphere and makes breathing difficult. But the priest in Hélder Câmara, who knows all about these things and is made anxious—yes, anxious!—by them, *also* sees in these signs of debilitation signs of hope as well.

He sees, for example, the growing disgust and resistance of public opinion to the arms race; the ever growing number of groups dedicated to nonviolence; the attempts to change structures not *for* the people but *with* the people; the attempts to tame the multinationals by working from within them. He points out that there are more and more chairs or departments of socio-political justice in the universities of many countries; that everywhere the weak are beginning to band together with the weak; that the hope of stemming selfishness is, on the whole, not lesser now but greater. In this outlook of his the archbishop seems to stand almost alone, and yet he is able, on point after point, to exclaim: "A clear sign of hope!"

For him as for John XXIII, all these are "signs of

God," accomplished in our age of hopelessness by the Lord who stands over all and acts in all and in everything.

The supposition is, of course, that there are individuals to whom has been given the gift of "the discernment of spirits"—a gift that Cardinal Lercaro (the "red" bishop of Bologna, who died in 1978) claimed for bishops above all others. It seems to me that the gift has been given to Helder Camara, and for this I thank God.

Mario von Galli

I

The Stirring of Hope

The Lord is there.
He is far less likely
to abandon us
in hardship
than in times of ease.

PUT YOUR EAR TO THE GROUND

Put your ear to the ground
and listen,
hurried, worried footsteps,
bitterness, rebellion.
Hope
hasn't yet begun.
Listen again.
Put out feelers.
The Lord is there.
He is far less likely
to abandon us
in hardship
than in times of ease.

HOPE WITHOUT RISK

Hope without risk
is not hope,
which is believing
in risky loving,
trusting others
in the dark,
the blind leap
letting God take over.

A SPARK OF HOPE

If only we would stop dividing ourselves.
If only humanity would stop producing and stockpiling
    the arms that someday will probably obliterate
    human life.
If only we could see that in place of all this fear
    and anxiety,
    in the most difficult and dark hours,
    in the darkest night, a star shines.
If only we, as brothers and sisters in greatness and misery,
    could find again
    a spark of hope.

GO DOWN

Go down
into the plans of God.
Go down
deep as you may.
Fear not
for your fragility
under that weight of water.
Fear not
for life or limb
sharks attack savagely.
Fear not the power
of treacherous currents under the sea.
Simply, do not be afraid.
Let go. You will be led
like a child whose mother
holds him to her bosom
and against all comers is his shelter.

II

Hope in Suffering

When I meet hearts that are like sponges stiff with chalk, how I would like to plunge into the water of God's infinite goodness!

WE CAN CHANGE OUR LIVES

The stone suffers
because all speak
of its hardness. . . .
And yet
You used to look for a stone
as a pillow for your head,
for you knew and you know
that the hope of stones
is to serve. . . .
When they serve
they become as soft
as clouds. . . .

Have you ever seen a dry sponge full of chalk dust? Have you ever held in your hand a dry sponge stiff with chalk? If you dip it in water, all the hardness disappears, all the stiffness vanishes.

When I meet hearts that are like sponges stiff with chalk, how I would like to plunge into the water of God's infinite goodness!

One day a lady, a dear friend of mine, said to me: "I'd be quite happy if my heart were like a sponge stiff with chalk. My case is worse. My heart has turned to stone. What good is a petrified heart?''

There are moments when words come to us that we did not know we had, unforeseen words, breathed directly into us by the Spirit of God. I repeated her words and commented on them: ''What good is your heart that has turned to stone? It's marvelous! Magnificent! Christ says he does not have even a stone on which to lay his head. Offer him your 'stone.' ''

The next day my friend said to me: ''Yesterday evening your words about Jesus not having even a stone on which to lay his head made me say to him: 'I find this a bit awkward. But if it's true that you are looking for a stone on which to lay your head, well, I have my stone here. It's a real joy for me to serve you, even in such a poor way.' ''

And she continued: ''I had an utterly deep sleep— something very rare for me. And the next day my heart no longer felt like a stone. I could look at everyone—even those who hate me and do me evil and are paid back with even stronger hate from me—I could look at everyone and almost sing for joy and peace.''

Where has the pessimism gone? The cold, dead questions; where are they? The ''What good is it? What good is it?''

Let us keep hoping! We can change our lives, transform our hearts!

Let us keep hoping! We can change our lives, transform our hearts!

WE CAN CONTROL OUR TIDES AND OUR MOONS

My interior tides and moods:
I love to see you change
—high tides and low tides
—waxing moon and waning moon
—new moon and full moon.
You help to overcome monotony.
But, dear low tide
and dear waning moon,
remain in my most secret self.
Out of love for hope,
take care,
tide and moon, my sisters,
to show yourself always,
to those especially who seek encouragement,
in your most encouraging form!

If you watch the changing high tides and low tides, you will surely discover that we too have our low tides and our high tides.

If you watch the changing phases of the moon—full moon, new moon, waxing moon, waning moon—you will undoubtedly discover that we too have our quarters like the moon. We have days when the moon wanes and days when it waxes, days when the moon is new and days when it is full. We even have our moonless nights.

Who can keep themselves always at high tide? Who can boast that they live always under a full moon?

Happy those among us who do all they can to overcome and keep those around—at home, at work, anywhere—from suffering the consequences of their low tides and their waning moons.

It is unjust and ungrateful to sulk and tighten the screw, to stir up the inner rage and then burst out against everyone. And yet how often we find ourselves bursting out most explosively at those who are the closest to us!

Has trouble arisen at work or on the way to it? Some inconvenience been inflicted? Is something very distasteful on the horizon? Some danger sending its signals ahead? Instead of the husband's trusting his wife enough to discuss these problems at home with her, he falls into a stubborn silence and explodes at the first excuse.

True enough, some husbands may object: "I've tried dialogue at home, with my wife. Impossible! She doesn't listen. She understands nothing. She rears up on all fours."

How much could be accomplished by a little good will on both sides!

There are individuals who even at low tide work the miracle of seeming always to be at high tide.

There are individuals who even when the moon is waning work the wonder of seeming to live under a waxing moon or even a full moon!

It is very advisable to examine our own face every morning, every evening, every night. Is it clouded over and threatening a storm? Is it bitter, distrustful, sad?

It is important to keep a firm grasp of this truth: bitterness, harshness, sadness are feelings that weaken us. They do harm. Instead of helping us face our problems, they only make the situation worse.

We can preserve interior peace! We can drive all bitterness, all resentment, from our minds and hearts!

We can struggle to preserve joy! We can maintain hope!

NEVER TO FALL IS NOT THE IMPORTANT THING

Thank you, Lord,
that your grace
helps us to realize
that rebellion
against weakness, sins, mistakes
is the pride
of those who think themselves perfect
and forget that we are
weakness, weakness, weakness!
Ah! If only our pride understood
that you perform miracles
to sustain
true and genuine humility.

The important thing is to begin again, humbly and courageously, after every fall.

When the not truly humble fall, they are crushed. "How could I possibly have fallen? It's unbelievable! How shameful! I cannot accept it!"

The truly humble laugh at themselves without any bitterness. No surprise. No astonishment. The important

15

thing is not to waste any time in standing up and beginning anew.

At the great judgment the Lord may say to someone: "How horrible! You fell a million times!" But all is salvaged if that person can say: "Yes, Lord, it really is frightful! But your grace helped me to get back on my feet quickly a million and one times!"

Did you pay attention to what I said a few lines above: The humble laugh at themselves without any bitterness? To laugh *with* others is fine. To laugh *at* yourself without bitterness, that's also fine. But never laugh *at* others!

To be untempted is not the important thing. The important thing is not to fall into temptation. Temptation is a call to stumble, an attraction to falling.

But along with bad temptations there are also good temptations: calls from on high! Calls to walk in faith, in love of God and God's creation, especially our fellow human beings.

They are calls to get up again and walk in hope.

HOPE FOR DESPAIRING YOUTH

It is not difficult to understand why. Later the young people of today will be better understood than they are. Their splendid values will be acknowledged and their faults will be seen as partly caused by us adults.

Let us try and see this young man sleeping in the airport lounge at Los Angeles. He is a North American. He has just come back from Vietnam. The untidy uniform betrays that this adolescent is not a born soldier. He was taken from university and had a machine gun put into his hands. He was sent half bewildered to Vietnam and forced to kill in order not to be killed. With total repugnance he must have pulled the trigger and killed for no reason young men like himself.

How can we be surprised if he turned to drugs to deaden his feelings? . . . He has come back from an absurd war—and what war is not absurd?—and he has not been welcomed with flowers. Nearly everyone looks at him with a sort of contemptuous pity. His girlfriend does not want to see him any more. His younger brothers do not want to hear about his feats of war and laugh at his medals.

Everywhere, in both rich and poor countries, there are many extraordinary young people, full of hope and generosity, ready to give all they value most to build a better world.

His parents wonder how he can be got back into ordinary life. . . .

Now try to imagine a room with dim lights in a country house. About twenty young men and women, knowing that in winter the house is left empty and shut up, have got hold of the key. The house belongs to one of the girls' parents. For three days and nights they smoke and try to dance, smoke and try to talk, smoke and try to get excited. Suddenly the owner of the house appears and finds them sitting, crashed out or asleep, their eyes closed or open and staring wildly. She had intended to throw them out and force her daughter to come home with her. But the sight is so painful that she dare not throw any of them out. She is overcome and sits on the ground among these young people in distress and bursts into tears.

If they dared speak, of course none of them could justify their suicidal behavior. But they would all make clear that they did not just smoke for the sake of smoking. They feel what seems to them the absurdity of life. They find no cause worthy of their youth and strength and they try to forget them.

It would be easy to give more examples. We could also mention young people, some almost children, who lose patience and engage in armed struggle. But as well as this, everywhere, in both rich and poor countries, there are many extraordinary young people, full of hope and generosity, ready to give all that they value most to build a better world.

Young men and women, the world is also young. The Abrahamic minorities are open to all, but you have a special place in them.

HOPE IN THE MIDST
OF SUFFERING

> Lord, when the cross
> falls on us full force
> it crushes us. . . .
> When you come
> along with the cross
> you embrace us. . . .

It is very easy for someone in good health to speak of the beauty and riches of suffering. God loves in a special way the person who clings to grace and almost joyfully (or even joyfully) accepts sufferings that are sometimes very difficult to bear.

A friend of mine was fully engaged in work not only *for* the poor but *with* the poor. Just when his heroic dedication was at its most intense, he became paralyzed on one side, like someone half dead. I came to see him and was afraid I would find him bitter, perhaps disillusioned: Was this semiparalysis the reward for his practical, heroic love of neighbor?

With an amiable smile he said: "I've begun to move out; half is already gone," and he pointed to the side of his body that was motionless.

A very beautiful friend of mine had fallen ill. She asked me as her confessor to pay her a visit.

She lay in bed, allowing only half of her face to be seen. With a smile she said: "Summon up your courage and don't be frightened." Then she showed me the other half of her face, terribly eaten by cancer.

I stood there in shock. How could cancer have been so insolent as to mar such beauty? Still smiling, she asked me to celebrate holy Mass there in her bedroom, because she wanted to unite her poor little suffering to the infinite suffering of God's Son, Jesus our brother.

We can grow, mature, enrich ourselves through suffering. We can continue to hope in the midst of suffering!

HOPE IN THE MIDST
OF WRETCHEDNESS

> Severina, when you said
> no money in the world
> could buy you
> your eyes and ears,
> your voice and breath,
> your mouth that eats and speaks,
> your arms, your feet, your legs,
> your head and your heart
> and, above all, your faith,
> I saw in you
> one truly rich
> with genuine wealth!

A friend of mine, who had come over from France, wanted to visit a slum.

When we arrived at a shantytown that truly deserved the terrible description "subhuman," I asked a courageous old lady named Severina to help us on our tour.

When the visit was over and my friend was ready to leave, she observed: "Lord! What wretchedness!"

When Severina caught the French word *misère* (which is

"I have riches that all the money in the world cannot buy: my eyes, my ears, my nose, my mouth, my hands, my arms, my feet, my legs, my head, my heart! And, above all, my faith!"

very like the Brazilian word for wretchedness: *miséria*),
she asked me: "Did I hear the lady talk of wretchedness?
Please tell her I realize how terrible conditions are in our
shantytown. Perhaps our *favela* does deserve to be called
'wretched.' But I do not consider myself to be in any way
wretched. I have riches that all the money in the world
cannot buy: my eyes, my ears, my nose, my mouth, my
hands, my arms, my feet, my legs, my head, my heart!
And, above all, my faith! This faith I would not exchange
or sell for all the money in all the banks of the world!"

Severina spoke with neither pride nor hatred. But I
could see that the visitor's words had unintentionally
touched a sensitive nerve: her deepest conviction, her reason for living, her wealth!

"Where your treasure is, there your heart will be!"

I was tempted to challenge Severina a bit—out of sheer
joy at "touching with our hands" so deep and beautiful a
treasure of life here "in the midst of wretchedness." I was
tempted to probe and find out how she had imbibed a conviction that is not so readily found where riches are
measured and weighed according to the millions and billions stored up in banks. But I left my foolish questions
unspoken.

Severina continues to be a sign of hope.

HOPE IN THE FACE
OF PERSECUTION

John Paul II,
this John beloved of God,
said in Brazil:
"I should a thousand times rather have
a persecuted church
than a church of compromises."

Annonciade is a poor woman of northeastern Brazil. She can neither read nor write. But she lives her faith, she lives the love of God and neighbor.

She lives in one of those many *favelas*—shantytowns—that provide visitors to our cities with the spectacle not of genuine growth but rather of a kind of bloatedness. Waves of the poor are continually reaching our cities. They come from the interior, from the rural world. There they led a subhuman life, but one more or less possible. The owners of the *latifundia*—great landed estates—allowed poor families to build hovels on their lands and gave them a little patch of ground on which to grow the absolute minimum of food for themselves. Of course, everyone had to work on the estates.

Today various circumstances have brought about a new situation:

- To increase production the owners of the estates have introduced powerful machines that require only a few skilled workers to run them. The majority of the peasants are left without work, but the land they occupied must now produce a greater yield.
- In other instances, the owners of the estates find it more profitable to drive away all those who used to live on their lands and put cattle in their place.
- There is also the alliance—and what an alliance!—between the great multinational corporations that have appeared on the scene and the small group of the indigenous wealthy. After all, the world is hungry and farming must be modernized!
- Food is becoming a strategic weapon like arms or oil! Powerful machines do the work of tens and even hundreds of workers. There is no question, of course, of producing food for the local population; the food is for export to the world's supermarkets.
- Governments plunge into gigantic building programs worthy of the pharaohs: breathtaking roads, splendid for those who have cars capable of doing 140 kilometers an hour; the most powerful hydro-electric plants in the world; the most extensive and sophisticated processing of such raw materials as gold, iron, uranium. . . .

When the poor families from the interior are driven away, they head for the cities, under the illusion that they will find work there—well-paying work!—and that they will find schools there for the children, hospitals for the sick, and—according to common report—housing for themselves. After looking in vain for the city of their dreams, all they can do is build their poor hovels or sub-hovels in the swamps, on hills of moving earth, or in places intended for streets or squares.

At other times they build on undeveloped land that sooner or later will be appraised. Then one day one of the so-called owners appears or a local government official with the police. The residents are driven out.

Let us go back to Annonciade's story. When the *favela* in which she was living was threatened with destruction, she tried to talk with each of her neighbors and encourage them to unite—peacefully, without weapons, without ha-tred or violence—in defense of one of the human crea-ture's fundamental rights: a place to live.

Emerging from the "house" of one of her neighbors, she saw the police car standing in front of her own.

Later on she commented: "It's almost impossible for someone who isn't poor to imagine what the police mean to the poor. The rich have lawyers and money to protect them. The poor have nothing.

"I was thrown into the police car and there I kept trem-bling shamefully. I felt a terrible chill. I kept saying to myself: 'My God! I didn't realize that I am so weak. I'm going to betray you. I'm going to act worse than Judas, worse than St. Peter. Help me, Christ! It's not my own self-esteem that's at stake. Or perhaps it is, just a little. But mainly to encourage my neighbors.'

"Just at that moment," Annonciade continued, "I re-membered a saying of Christ that I had heard at a 'Meet your Brothers and Sisters' gathering, which is an experiment in liberating evangelization in which the poor are instructed and evangelized by the poor. Christ said: 'When you are brought before the tribunal, don't worry about the answers you are to give. The Spirit of the Lord will speak in your stead.' "

During that ride Annonciade kept thinking of these words and, still trembling and weak from her chill, kept saying: "You said that, Lord! Keep your promise."

When she came before the interrogator, who could easily have crushed her or caused her to disappear—as so many others have disappeared for good, with the excuse that they might have escaped from prison or caused an uprising in prison—she gave answers so powerful and so beautiful that later on she could not repeat them.

Once again, as Christ had promised, the Spirit of God spoke through Annonciade.

III

Signs of God in a Hopeless Time

You need not feel isolated, you need not be discouraged, when you are trying to revitalize the institution itself from within.

ARE INSTITUTIONS HOPELESS?

One of the temptations that face the Abrahamic minorities is the fear that the structures of which they are part make it impossible for them to have any real effect in changing the world. They are tempted because they do not feel they are better than other people.

For example priests or nuns who want to follow the spirit of Vatican II or bring into effect the conclusions of the Latin American bishops' conference at Medellín should not be astonished if they feel misunderstood by their brothers and sisters. They would be yielding to temptation if they decided to leave their community and give way to dangerous bitterness.

Instead of feeling beaten, instead of quitting and imagining how to reform the institution from the outside, would it not be better to think that within the institution itself and in all sorts of places there are others who are in the middle of the very same experience? Why not seek an intelligent and effective way, which would also be loyal and constructive, of contacting all these others who are also anxious to serve their neighbor better? I do not mean condemning those who are more conservative or plotting against them. I mean you need not feel isolated, you need not be discouraged, when you are trying to revitalize the institution itself from within.

Of course you will risk being misunderstood. However pure your intentions you will look like a rebel. Perhaps you will be punished. This is excellent training for attacking and overcoming socio-economic and politico-cultural structures. You will be able to take the measure of your courage, prudence, loyalty, kindness, power of decision and responsibility.

Similar situations also arise in the protestant churches. Protestants following the gospel and the conclusions of the Uppsala or Bayreuth congresses, and wanting to bring peace through justice and work for a true education for freedom, may also feel hampered. People are shocked and suspicious of them. They are regarded as "advanced" or even "crypto-communist". They think that these judgments on them are against the gospel. They are scandalized and angry and think they will have to leave their church in order to remain faithful to Christ.

Many clergy and lay people are likewise tempted. However right and necessary it is to attack the faults of these institutions, it is a grave mistake to think they can simply be wiped out for a fresh start to be made. It is impossible to live outside a minimum structure or organization. Unfortunately even those structures which are most effective and reasonable to begin with always become intolerable after a while.

Everyone should realize that there are other young people, and adults, everywhere who want what they want. . . . Minorities in every group could form a nucleus for the greater service of others and all these minorities united could become an irresistible force.

Young buddhists, shintoists, moslems, jews, catholics and atheists all have the same reactions today to their own srtuctures. This advice is for all of them: be aware of the temptation and take steps to overcome it.

Other structures also repress instead of encouraging initiative. Doctors and nurses are sometimes deprived of the most basic equipment for their work. Teachers some-times have nowhere for their pupils to sit. Social workers spend time working out large projects but are not given the means even to put small projects into practice. All these people should realize that they are not alone in their desire to serve their neighbor more effectively. There are minori-ties everywhere with the same desire. It would be easy to give further examples, among workers, peasants, journal-ists, soldiers, etc. . . . There are Abrahamic minorities everywhere who are only waiting for the signal to begin and to unite.

HOPE AND FRUSTRATION
OF HUMAN DIALOGUE

Holy Father, let humankind,
as it cuts loose
from its tiny earth
and little galaxy,
discover at last
how ridiculous are
its vanity and pride
and how stupid it has been
so far
in its pretenses at dialogue.

In their life and activity, the white peoples are driven by a conscious or unconscious racism: they are the ones capable of bringing about progress (today called development), building an advanced civilization, giving the example of a superior culture and of true religion.

The white peoples therefore believe they have an obligation to help the nonwhite peoples—black, yellow, red. Otherwise, left to themselves, they would, it is thought, remain forever backward.

The first extensive attempt at dialogue and aid came during the time of the "discoveries."

The "discoverers" stumbled upon millions of natives, peoples with colored skin. In their vanity the whites claimed that those natives did not exist previously. Their official existence began once they had been "discovered."

Indigenous cultures were unhesitatingly destroyed. The natives themselves had to choose between slavery and wars of annihilation. In keeping with the outlook of the times, native peoples who accepted enslavement had to accept baptism as a consolation and a challenge.

The second major attempt at dialogue and help was colonization.

The cultures of the indigenous nonwhite peoples were crushed, usually in indirect and subtle ways. Even more indirect and subtle were enslavement and the obligation of living as Christians. But worst of all for the nonwhite peoples was the help given to the "colonies"; everyone knows what negative results this had.

The third major attempt at dialogue and help was the coming of the multinational corporations among nonwhite peoples.

The multinationals claim that they come in order to bring new technologies, a stable currency, and many new jobs. In practice, there is economic growth for a minuscule minority of rich natives who form a natural alliance with the incoming multinationals. For the nonwhite peoples as a whole there is an increase in foreign debt and a minimum of new jobs, because modern technologies reduce to a minimum the number of workers needed and because such

Despite the present situation, in which more than two-thirds of the human race are reduced to a subhuman condition of wretchedness and hunger, there are clear signs of hope among both the nonwhite and the white peoples.

workers as are required need a technical training that is too advanced for the nonwhite indigenes.

Destruction of native cultures? Enslavement? Yes. Not openly and officially, however, but indirectly and subtly.

But this time, and increasingly, the church no longer helps in pseudodialogue. Instead, without hatred or violence but also without fear, it denounces the injustices that are crushing more and more millions of God's children.

Despite the present situation, in which more than two-thirds of the human race are reduced to a subhuman condition of wretchedness and hunger, there are clear signs of hope among both the nonwhite and the white peoples.

Here are some paths of hope that must be examined more closely and understood more profoundly:

Among the Third World peoples:

- The small basic communities in which persons gather not in order to trample on the rights of others but in order to keep their own rights from being trampled on.
- A religion that is practiced without being imposed from outside, does not cause alienation, and is found to be a source of hope and liberation.
- Among social workers who want to be of real help, the happy experience of working not only *for* the people but *with* the people.

Among the First World peoples:

- Small groups, especially of the young, who are determined to help create a more just and human world. In

Europe these groups already number over fifteen hundred; they have an international secretariat (Pax Christi International) and have already held a number of international congresses. They follow a clear and courageous policy of active nonviolence and are perfecting an increasingly effective method: moral pressure in behalf of liberation.

- The discovery of a number—far larger than had been thought—of men and women of good will who need only to be properly instructed and have their consciences touched—and they will help bring liberating moral pressure to bear.

- The situation worldwide, which is becoming daily more absurd and drawing closer to universal suicide, and demands with increasing urgency that present socio-economic structures be radically changed.

- The attitude of the scientists and the experts who run the technologies, including electronics, and who in bringing ever more wealth to small minorities are bringing wretchedness to almost the whole of the human race; these scientists and experts are now engaged in impressive efforts to appreciate and safeguard what is truly human in themselves and their lives.

- The world religions, which are drawing closer together and looking more to what unites them than to what separates them, and which feel responsible not only for the life to come but for helping to create justice and love in this world as the indispensable way to a true and lasting peace.

HOPE AND THE MADNESS
OF THE ARMS RACE

Lord Jesus, at your arrest,
when your companion
put his hand on his sword,
drew it,
struck the servant on the ear
and cut it off,
you said to him:
"Put your sword back in its scabbard,
for all
who take the sword
will perish by the sword."
What do you say
to the making and use
of nuclear arms?

Groups dedicated to active nonviolence often organize
demonstrations to help persons of good will realize in
some measure the madness of the arms race. They remind
us that governments today (led by the United States and
the Soviet Union) spend $1 million on the arms race every
minute—$450 billion every year.

At the same time they point out all that could be built and bought with this money: how many schools and hospitals, how much food.

Alongside photographs of Hiroshima and Nagasaki are photographs of present-day nuclear missiles.

When a new Trident submarine leaves harbor with its cargo of twenty missiles, it has the power to annihilate 410 cities the size of Hiroshima and Nagasaki.

We are aware that computer errors could lead to a nuclear war.

SIPRI (the Stockholm International Peace Research Institute) provides key information for conscientization with regard to the arms race. Do you know how many countries have nuclear installations, supposedly for peaceful purposes? Do you know for sure whether it is easy or difficult to convert from peaceful use to military use? Do you know with accuracy how many agreements on the control of nuclear weapons reduce the number of such weapons but at the same time allow for a frightful increase in their destructive power?

The manufacture of armaments is so expensive that nations, besides providing them for themselves, must also produce them for sale, in order to mitigate the horrendous pressure of military budgets on national economies. But the United States and the Soviet Union have no need to buy weapons. The two superpowers have sixty times what they need for the total destruction of life on our planet.

Weaponry is sold to countries that do not have even the minimum needed for supplying the necessities of life to their own people.

Weapons share the same characteristics as other products of consumer societies: they are irresistible to buyers and yet become quickly outmoded.

On the other hand, if arms sellers come a second and third time with new wares on the grounds that the old are outmoded, and if meanwhile a nuclear war has not broken out, buyers will soon say that such a war is a bugaboo thought up by sellers.

The least that can be said of the countries that manufacture weapons is that they should be happy to learn that a war has broken out in the countries that buy them. This is the *least* that can be said.

All men and women of good will are therefore urged to combat the madness of the arms race by marshaling public opinion in every way possible against the manufacture and proliferation of arms.

Peaceful, impressive demonstrations against the nuclear arms race, like that of the hundred thousand persons in Hamburg, must become more numerous.

And there you have a *clear sign of hope*!

HOPE AND THE IDEOLOGY
OF NATIONAL SECURITY

Shadrach, Meshach, and Abednego,
is it true
that states
that see National Security
as the supreme value
are like Nebuchadnezzar
with his golden statue
that the king commanded
to be adored?
Adoration today
consists in the idea that,
in defense of the supreme value,
everything is permissible:
kidnappings, tortures,
disappearances, murders.
Everything is permissible
to safeguard
National Security.
Is this
when one must be willing
to be cast
into the fiery furnace?

Clearly, the Spirit of God
inspires a new song
that will encourage
the victims
of the idolatries of every age.

When violence reaches the point of absurdity it begins to create in some countries a kind of nostalgia for strong government. Many citizens become concerned about National Security. The impression often arises that the worst threat, now as always, is that posed by communist aggression.

For many individuals the knowledge that the Soviet Union possesses sixty times the weapon-power needed to eradicate life from the earth becomes a terrible nightmare. The same knowledge about the United States brings a sigh of relief and gratitude. And the desire grows to strengthen National Security by strengthening, for example, the North Atlantic Treaty Organization.

No one can overlook the fact that both capitalism and communism are well skilled in exploiting the opposition between them. But they are also skilled—very much so, indeed—in walking hand in hand when their interests make it advisable.

How can we forget that during the Second World War the Allies worked together with the Soviet Union to conquer Nazism? This collaboration came about quickly, with no loss of time. Then, when the war was over, Roosevelt, Stalin, and Churchill at Yalta divided the world into spheres of influence. They dismembered Germany and even the city of Berlin.

How is it possible to avoid seeing that, as the century

draws to its close, the real confrontation is not between East and West but between North and South?

Today, the great multinationals, the darling progeny of capitalism, are installed in Russia itself, and this includes the banking system.

The multinationals simply waited for the death of Mao Tse-tung in order to gain entry into China.

Given this confused situation as far as East and West, North and South are concerned, it is a *clear sign of hope* to find ever more numerous groups dedicated to active non-violence. They are convinced that:

- The decisive confrontation of this century is between North and South—that is, between a small group of countries that grow ever richer because they unjustly oppress almost the entire human race, and the oppressed who already number more than two-thirds of the world population.

- Although a people may legitimately make provision for its self-defense, to make National Security the supreme value is first and foremost an act of idolatry. The harsh experience of Latin America shows that when National Security is made the value of values, the supreme value, everything becomes permissible in its support: kidnappings, torture, disappearances of persons, assassinations, dictatorships.

- After the all too bitter experience of Latin America, which derived its ideology from North America, men and women of good will must be awakened to see the danger of allowing the National Security ideology to spread.

Although a people may legitimately make provision for its self-defense, to make National Security the supreme value is first and foremost an act of idolatry. The harsh experience of Latin America shows that when National Security is made the value of values, the supreme value, everything becomes permissible in its support: kidnappings, torture, disappearances of persons, assassinations, dictatorships.

HOPE AND THE WASTE OF RAW MATERIALS

My brothers and sisters,
the Lord
has given us a share
in divine understanding
and creative power.
The Lord was humble and bold enough
to bid us
control nature
and complete the creation.
Have we, then, the right
to pollute nature
and destroy it
by wasting raw materials
that cannot be replaced?
My brothers and sisters,
we must learn
from the Lord God
to create and not destroy.
Destruction
is unworthy of the creator,
and even more of the co-creator.

The industrial countries are beginning to realize that their survival depends on the Third World. We need only recall the German report on manganese, molybdenum, asbestos, chromium, and vanadium. If these five raw materials could not be had, it would be catastrophic for the aircraft, shipbuilding, automobile, and iron industries.

We can easily imagine what would happen to the industrial countries in their entirety if all the raw materials extracted from the Third World and wasted by the consumer societies (wasteful societies!) were suddenly withheld from the industrialized world.

It is a fact that the countries in which the raw materials originate depend on the industrial countries, because through advertising the latter have created false needs in the former. If the Third World had enough sense and courage to free itself from the prejudices created by the refined comforts they have imported from abroad, the underdeveloped countries could engage in their own kind of development, a slower but perhaps happier kind. What has happened in the case of oil should set us thinking.

The price of raw materials—and not simply the price of industrial products—was always determined in the great decision-making centers of the world. During the twenty great years of the auto industry, the price of gasoline rose hardly at all.

But when the oil-producing countries banded together and tried to fix the price of their raw material, the industrial world was frightened. The rich nations in the northern half of our planet were shocked: What if other producers of raw materials followed the example of the oil producers?

In all honesty, however, who profits by even nonexorbitant prices for raw materials? The answer is clear proof of what has been claimed by many for a long time—namely, that in the countries that produce raw materials there is a tiny minority of wealthy nationals who maintain their wealth at the cost of their fellow citizens. They are the indigenous allies of the multinational newcomers.

Take the example of oil:

- It is said that even in the glorious days of OPEC the multinational oil corporations took 75 percent of the new profits.
- In the oil-producing countries the minority that controls the oil shows no concern for the masses who continue to live in subhuman conditions. Meanwhile the owners of the oil give the impression of not knowing what to do with the new oil money and they make a show of themselves with crazy and ridiculous expenditures.

The Third World will always be vulnerable as long as it is manipulated by local minorities—elites imposing internal colonialism in their respective countries.

Nonetheless, here again there is a *clear sign of hope*:

- In the Third World countries there are small groups, especially of the young, who instead of simply working *for* the people work *with* the people.
- These groups are convinced that the human advancement of the masses that subsist in subhuman conditions can and must be encouraged and helped.

There is in fact no other way of obtaining truly human advancement: either it will be accomplished by the oppressed themselves or it will never be more than a dream, an illusion.

HOPE OF THE WATER
AND THE STONES

Water, dear child
of your Father and our Father,
lives in hope
of serving.
It knows
that in serving
it becomes dirty
to our human eyes.
But in God's eyes it is transfigured.
To serve in this way
is to be enriched
in the eyes of God
and in your eyes.

HOPE AND THE MULTINATIONALS

A multinational
for augmenting the domination
of a third—and even less than a third—
over the other two-thirds
—and even more than two-thirds—
of the human race
reduced to a subhuman state
of wretchedness and hunger?
No!

A multinational
of faith,
of love,
of hope?
Yes!

The mushrooming development of technology in our
ay—now doubled, tripled, and even quadrupled by the
ectronic revolution—practically requires that production
e on a multinational, worldwide scale.
This fact would already be enough to establish the

power of the great multinational corporations; they have become established in dozens of countries.

But their power is based above all on the alliances they are able to set up:

• With military forces:

Before General Eisenhower, a man above suspicion, left the White House after his second term, he courageously denounced the danger in his own country of the alliance between economic power and military power.

The army needs money for the arms race and for spy satellites. The great corporations gain the protection of the military.

Today this kind of alliance is no longer peculiar to the United States.

• With the great communications media:

It is so expensive today to run a modern newspaper or magazine, a modern radio station and especially a modern television station, an advertising agency or a press agency, that they can hardly carry on and survive without the help of the multinationals. And it is obvious that once they are given help, there will be compromise—clever and subtle— demanded of the media.

• With the great universities:

Without research there is no university. But genuine research is so expensive that the universities need the support of foundations. And behind the foundations is the money of the multinationals. . . .

With the intelligence agencies:

It is not enough simply to know the local market possibilities. It is also necessary to know the degree of understanding, the good or bad will, the readiness to cooperate with multinationals, on the part of governments, political groups, churches, labor unions, basic communities. There are multinationals that do not hesitate to support or overthrow governments, depending on their attitudes to the multinationals, who seek entrance in order—so they claim—to bring new technologies, a stable currency, and many new jobs.

But despite the apparently insuperable power of the multinationals and the great danger created by the alliances they make, there are *clear signs of hope.*

There are groups of young persons to be found in many countries who share a single idea: to bring moral pressure to bear on the multinationals through inquiries, the spreading of information, and lawsuits. Here is an example, in summary form, of the kind of things they do.

A group of young persons managed through personal sacrifices to get enough money together to buy shares in a great multinational corporation of their country. This gave them the right to take part in the annual general meeting of the enterprise. They also managed to get a list of stockholders. To each they wrote a letter that read something like this:

We are your colleagues, because we have shares in this great corporation. As shareholders, we all want to make a profit, of course. But we are sure that you do not want a profit that demands the crushing of human beings.

Clearly, it is more convenient simply to buy shares, ask no significant questions of the directors of the corporation, and then at the end of the year receive the largest possible profit from the treasurer's office.

This time we ask you to make a personal sacrifice and attend the annual meeting, and when there pay close attention not just to what is said in general but to the facts presented, the information, the statistics that show that you are being asked to accept profit that is stained by human blood.

The directors quickly changed one of the regulations to require that anyone wishing to address the annual meeting must own a certain minimum number of shares (the excuse: to keep the meeting from becoming too long!). As a result, the group of young persons could get no further.

But now religious groups are trying, across confessional borders (e.g., the Interfaith Center for Corporate Responsibility, in the United States), to bring to bear on the great multinational corporations the liberating moral pressure that the group of young persons had planned but could not carry out because they had too few shares.

HOPE OF OVERCOMING SELFISHNESS

Break through your shell of selfishness.
If you do not
know yourself,
you will never know
others.
Selfishness
is the deepest root
of all unhappiness
—your own and
—that of the whole world.
It feeds an insatiable hunger
that first eats up
everything belonging to others
and then causes a creature
to devour itself.

The Creator and Father willed that the human person—
creature—should be a co-creator, a sharer in the divine
nderstanding and creative power, and should be commis-
ioned to control nature and complete creation.

As far as understanding is concerned, humankind has

Human beings will learn at last—always with God's help—to control their selfishness or even liberate themselves from it for good.

lways accepted its role as co-creator; it has always paid
onor to God's boldness and humility in raising a creature
o a divine level. When humankind discovered fire or the
wheel, it was honoring the Creator, just as it was when it
egan space flight and reached the moon.

But as for selfishness—how primitive, backward, and
idiculous this pitiable co-creator shows itself to be!

All we need to do is remind ourselves of the condition of
he world in an age when we are tapping the potential of
uclear energy and making the incredible discoveries that
lectronics promises for the near future. What is the condi-
ion of the world? More than two-thirds of the human race
s living in subhuman conditions of wretchedness and
unger!

Only the goodness of the Creator can so touch the mind
nd heart of humankind as to enable it to overcome its
wn selfishness. But the Creator uses human instruments
o spread the light and power that insight brings.

It is incredible: humankind still needs to be humanized!

Educators sought to humanize through humanism.
veryone knows the hopes they set on the study of Latin
nd Greek and of Greco-Roman literature.

In the age when the natural sciences were beginning their
emarkable advance, the Renaissance clung to instruction
n Latin and Greek as a humanizing force, but scientists set
heir hopes on science. They were convinced that as individuals advanced in scientific knowledge, they could not
ut also mature as human beings.

Humankind—thought the scientists—cannot logically
o other than become more human. It cannot but reject

the selfishness that keeps it from being fully human.

Both hopes have suffered shipwreck: the hope of the educators and the hope of the scientists.

Today, however, as the human race gains new and unexpected knowledge of the universe, the cosmos, it seems that human beings will learn at last—always with God's help—to control their selfishness or even liberate themselves from it for good.

Thanks to the most up-to-date instruments that can, for example, pick up radio waves from the most distant stellar spaces, the sister sciences of astronautics and astronomy are advancing with incredible rapidity and preparing surprises that, we hope, will do away with human selfishness. For:

- When we realize that, according to quite unequivocal indications, the number of inhabitable planets—previously estimated to be about 600 million—must in fact be far more numerous than that;

- When we realize that serious scientists are trying to establish laws governing the relationships of human beings with other beings at our level or with beings above or below our level;

- When we realize that the Christian faith sees no difficulty in the presence of life, even intelligent, free life at a human, superhuman, or subhuman level, scattered among millions and millions, perhaps even billions, of stars, and maintains only that the earth (this tiny earth) will forever have the glory and responsibility of having been gifted with the incarnation of God's Son, Jesus Christ;

If it seems difficult or even impossible to imagine that the Creator in infinite power and wisdom should have created billions of stars (millions of times larger than this tiny earth) simply so that they might abide in their measureless spaces and twinkle for us to feast our eyes on;

• If all this is so (and there can hardly be any doubt in view of the serious scientific arguments), and if we reflect even briefly on it all:

• *Then*, does not the earth become a little speck of dust following after the armies of the stars? Will humankind not become very modest, and will it not accept its task of responsibility as co-creator in a spirit of love and humility, a spirit of solidarity with the whole human race and even with all the life in the cosmos?

All of this becomes a *visible sign of hope* that we will see the human creation liberated from selfishness, for in the final analysis, selfishness is the chief cause of the injustices and unhappiness that the human race suffers.

But unless we pray to you, Father, and unless we have your help, this third attempt to humanize humankind will also be condemned to fail.

HOPE STRENGTHENED BY THE UNIVERSITIES

University, be on guard!
Do not let yourself
be cooped up
in your courses and programs
controlled directly or indirectly
by selfish and insatiable minorities
who lack the courage
to confront
the really great human problems
of our time.
If the young do not see you
open without fear
to truth,
to hope, to love,
they will exchange you
for the university of life!

It is fairly easy to show the folly of such things as the arms race (especially a nuclear arms race), or National Security as the supreme value, or the consumer society (the waste of society!), or the terrible injustices of international trade policies, or racism, or the emptiness of a onesided human dialogue, or the multinational corporations.

But it is evidently not enough simply to point out these follies. There is need of radical reflection on such serious problems as those just mentioned.

There is need to inquire in a scientific way whether there may not be something positive hidden in the problems I have characterized as follies. Is there really question of folly? If there is, is the folly total and beyond correction? Or is it possible to avoid the negative and promote the positive?

Will struggle against these follies lead to new ones— perhaps to follies even more burdensome and dangerous? If the follies I have mentioned are really calamities to be avoided, is it possible to indicate any alternatives, so that the approach may not remain purely negative?

Here, then, is another *clear sign of hope*:

Professorships, study centers, and seminars dealing with justice are multiplying in the universities. Their purpose is to investigate scientifically the questions and problems already mentioned and to create a fuller consciousness of them.

Even in the rich industrial countries it is a privilege to attend a university. In the Third World it is a privilege to attend a primary school, and a further privilege to attend it through to the final grades! It is privilege heaped upon privilege to attend a middle or secondary school, reach the university, and win an academic degree. There are university entrance examinations that are like battlefields: anyone hoping to get into a university must conquer eight, ten, or twelve competitors who will be left outside the door.

The thing that is lacking almost everywhere—in the Third World and in the industrialized world—is universities with the courage to face up to the really great human problems of our time.

Humanism, humane letters, anthropology—all the fine descriptive labels are there, but not the boldness needed to discuss such urgent problems as the ones I shall simply outline in what follows.

How are we to eliminate, peacefully but courageously, the great scandal of our century: that more than two-thirds of the human race is living in subhuman conditions of wretchedness and hunger?

Contemporary humankind knows how to eliminate earthly wretchedness; it has all the means and all the science needed. But is the struggle against wretchedness and the victory over it compatible with the arms race? Is it compatible with the wastefulness characteristic of the consumer society? With the fearful injustices of international trade policies? With National Security as the absolute and supreme value? With the great multinational corporations?

How is it possible, peacefully but effectively, to change the structures that continually augment the wealth of the rich and at the same time intensify untold wretchedness all over the world and drown almost the whole of humankind in it?

Professorships in justice are already established in various universities with the clearly and decisively formulated task of reflecting more deeply on such deplorable and explosive problems as the ones just mentioned.

Such university chairs in justice meet with very strong

nd even tenacious opposition. A university may easily be o pressured—financially or in terms of other responsibil- ies—that the only solution is to cancel the professorship r—what is worse and sadder—to reduce it to a colorless, feless chair of law, to a caricature of a true chair of jus- ice.

But hope does not die so easily.

If the various groups pursuing active nonviolence (their umber grows from year to year in all countries, especially n Europe) can unite in dealing with two or three of the nore important problems, they will be adequately sup- orted by all men and women of good will. All of them ogether can see to it that authentic chairs of justice be stablished. This will be an effective contribution to the earch for a true and lasting peace.

HOPE FROM THE ALLIANCE
OF THE WEAK WITH
THE WEAK

An alliance of the weak with the weak?
To the powerful and the superpowerful
it sounds ridiculous.
Has Goliath
forgotten David
who was hardly more than a child?

Among his parables Jesus Christ tells the story of the poor man Lazarus and the rich man. The rich man is being asphyxiated by his super-comfort and luxury, but the poor man Lazarus starves at the gate of the rich man's palace and asks in vain for the crumbs that fall from his table.

How could the parable have ended if the rich man had been conquered by grace and had called Lazarus and said to him: "Come, there is room for you at my table!"

The poor man would have been ashamed to enter the rich man's house, for he was dirty in clothing and body.

Many ask the poor to keep themselves clean. But cleanliness requires water (and at least in the Third World water is a luxury for the poor), a change of clothing, and houses in which to live.

But suppose that, encouraged by the rich man, Lazarus with his wounds did finally take his place at the table set almost daily with a banquet. How would he have summoned up the courage to talk with the rich host man-to-man as with a brother?

The poor, the weak, the oppressed come to the wealthy as beggars with hands outstretched. At least that is true of the two-thirds who live in subhuman conditions.

There is no question of telling the poor to turn to hatred and violence. If the poor were so foolish as to take up arms against the rich, they would be wiped out: weapons are manufactured by the rich oppressors of the people.

If an entire oppressed people were to start a war of liberation, it would have to ask help of a superpower other than the one dominating it. The superpower thus called on might come rushing in with arms and soldiers, and could help the oppressed win a victory. But it would be naive to think that the superpower would then return home. The excuse of having to safeguard the fruits of victory is more than enough to justify its remaining and becoming a new master.

If the rich countries of the North were to invite the countries of the Third World, the South, for a dialogue but were not to make their own intentions clear, it would be like the rich man of the gospel inviting Lazarus to his table for an impossible conversation.

A North-South dialogue presupposes truly fraternal North-South conversations. At the present time, however, when the South attends conferences or congresses or conversations, it is always represented by the wealthy elite from the poor countries. Thus the North makes a game out of dividing the South.

Yet here again there is a *visible sign of hope*: awareness of the need to help the poor of the South unite with the poor of the South. If the alliance—the solidarity of the weak with the weak—becomes a reality some day—and there is something of this now taking place—then and only then will there be a meaningful North-South dialogue.

Within the Third World, Latin America is not a bit wiser, better informed, or more competent than its likes, Africa and Asia. Nonetheless Latin America bears a heavy responsibility toward Africa and Asia.

Africa and Asia are a babel of languages and dialects, but all of Latin America speaks practically the same language—Spanish and Portuguese being so closely related.

Africa and Asia are a babel of religions, but the same Christian sensibilities predominate everywhere in Latin America.

In addition, Latin America has behind it over a century and a half of experiences of political (though not economic and cultural) independence; only today are many countries in Africa and Asia beginning to have this experience.

These conditions encourage Latin America to be a sign of hope inasmuch as young Latin Americans are determined, and are preparing themselves, to promote a genuine Latin American integration without at the same time promoting imperialism either foreign or domestic.

The goal is not a new economic bloc after the model of the European Common Market. There is no question of claiming a leadership role in the Third World so as to issue commands to fellow countries of Africa and Asia. No! A genuine Latin American integration is simply a good basis for an even more inclusive solidarity of the weak with the weak, and thus for a genuine and effective North-South dialogue.

> Father!
> Your Spirit told us
> through the mouth of Paul
> that the whole earth
> and we too
> as your children
> groan
> in the pains of a birth!
> It is easy, Lord,
> to grasp and affirm this.
> For there are passages
> so difficult
> and hours
> so filled with anguish
> that the image really applies:
> they are labor pains!
> Something is being born.
> Who knows?
>> A world in which men and women can breathe,
>> a more just, a more human world!

From the mingled light and shadow
of hope
I greet you, Lord, God.

THE BEGINNING OF THE BEGINNING OF THE DAY

Holy Father,
some day
the burden of today's toil
—the goings and comings,
    the successes and failures,
    the hopes and near despairs—
will all be transformed
into blessed reality!
Hope will be no more. . . .
I reach the point of near absurdity:
of thanking you that I live
during the difficult phase
in which hope is still
the beginning of the beginning
of the day!
Day
is still struggling,
and has many struggles ahead,
to be born!
From the mingled light and shadow
of hope
I greet you, Lord, God.

Why pray for the rich? All human beings are invited to share in your divine riches.

IV

Prayer for the Rich

Father,
pray for the rich?
Whence comes this sudden idea?
After all, Jesus, your Son and our brother,
was very hard on the rich.
He saw them as, humanly speaking,
beyond hope and beyond redemption.
He added only that for you
nothing is impossible—
even where human beings see no escape
and no solution.

Why pray for the rich
who have not only money
but power, intelligence, and talent?
Why pray even for those
who are rich in virtues and good deeds?
They already have everything.

They seem to have no need of your aid.
They are sufficient unto themselves.

Yet we must pray and beseech you
to let the scales fall from their eyes
so that they may at last see
that you alone are truly rich
because you alone have life,
knowledge and freedom,
and the fulness of holiness.
Of course, you have given us something of these.
You made humankind after your own image and
    likeness.
You commissioned it
to master the natural world
and bring creation to completion.
You give it a share of your divinity,
of your creative power.

How can we fail to understand
that it is theft
to clutch these gifts to ourselves
as if they had not been given on loan,
as if they could be the privilege of a few?
Whether or not the few realize it,
they are responsible
for the oppression of countless human beings,
and every day their vast numbers increase.

Lord,
help those who give themselves credit
for their riches.

These are the pitiable rich:
they do not attain to the simplicity
that knows everything is a gift
and to the comradely spirit
that never forgets all human beings are invited
to share in your divine riches.

Poor rich persons who must
suddenly, perhaps tomorrow,
realize with utter clarity, the illusion
in which they have been trapped!
They are like actors on the stage
who play the part of rich folk.
They behave like the rich,
talk like the rich,
are taken for the rich and received like the rich.
When the curtain falls,
the play is over:
do they then think
they have really become rich?

Help all those
who have made themselves rich,
even if perhaps through hard work:
convince them
that the best inheritance they can leave their children
is the living example
of justice,
of the open heart and the open hand,
of freedom from money
by using it for service
and not making an idol of it.

The best inheritance they can leave their children is the living example of justice, of the open heart and the open hand.

A checkbook cannot be taken with you
when you die.
In the presence of eternity
there is but one currency:
love in action, love that is lived.

Anyone who has become rich
must be warned:
families that once were united
begin to feud
when an inheritance is at stake.
The moment when an inheritance is divided
is not a good time;
all too often it is a dreadful time.

Help those who in the political world
have reached the pinnacle, or seeming pinnacle,
of power.
They regard themselves not only as powerful
but as born to demand
obedience, followers,
a ready hearing, and service.
They must realize
that Jesus, your Son and our brother, came
not to be served
but to serve.
Our age tolerates
power and authority
only when they favor dialogue and even lead dialogue.
All over the world
there is an effort to end

the division between people and power,
people and party.

Help the scientists, men of letters, and artists
who consider themselves wise and discerning.
Let them not lose their heads. . . .
Let them remain aware
that every advance in research is a tiny step
compared with what is yet to be discovered.
Scientific discoveries and surprises
follow in rapid succession;
machines process information and data.
This development should inspire humility
in scholars and intellectuals,
today more than ever before.

Technicians are the first to experience
the glory and shame of technology.
The glory: it is enough to recall
the spectacle seen by the entire world,
when from a little corner of the earth
technicians control space flights
down to the last detail;
changes of course and even
the breathing and blood circulations
of the voyagers are recorded.
Alongside the glory, the shame:
it is demeaning
to place spirit and specialized knowledge
in the service of a few, increasingly concentrated,
    undertakings.

In a special way, Lord,
scholars, technicians, artists, and intellectuals
share in your creative power.
Let them think of themselves
as co-creators
and derive their inspirations
from the one true source
of beauty, light, and truth.

Help your servants
who are entrusted with a spiritual office
and are commissioned
to perform the holiest of actions.
We priests
may not put distance between you and your people.
Let us be true *pontifices*, "bridge-builders."
The bridges we build must be
broad and passable,
so that everyone can reach you.

Only when we—
the church and each of us—
are not attached to
privileges, power, and money,
can we serve you fully.
Let us pour out our lives
in the service of our neighbor!
That is the best way
of serving you and observing
the one and only commandment:
love of God and humankind.

We priests may not put distance between you and your people. Let us be true pontifices, "bridge-builders." The bridges we build must be broad and passable, so that everyone can reach you.

Help those
who, through a strict life and active charity,
have won the reputation of saints,
yet are so weak,
to be even better men and women for their fellow
    humans.
They see themselves as just, pure, and holy.
Jesus, your Son and our brother,
was most understanding and generous
to all sinners
but hard on the Pharisees.
He attacked them openly,
fought them and urged his disciples
to do as they said but not as they did.

There is a dangerous and degenerate kind of wealth:
to be proud
of one's humility, poverty, and mortifications,
of one's mystical communion.

Lord, help those
who are always beginning anew
on the way of holiness
to persevere. The world needs saints.
Genuine holiness feeds incessantly
on humility and genuine love.

Help the young!
Theirs are the inexhaustible riches of the future.
They are masters of enthusiasm and hope.
They long to live in a world
without inferiors and superiors.

Father, you understand that when I say "youth"
I am not measuring it by years.
There are twenty-year-olds
who have no gray hairs or wrinkles
but are spiritless conformists.
And it is possible to be eighty-four
(I am thinking of Pope John XXIII)
and to have retained
a youthfulness of soul and heart.

The world has need
of the marvelous riches
we know as youth.

Let not an easy life corrupt the young,
let no difficulty discourage them.
And make them proof
against the worst danger of all:
the danger of settling down, of losing their fire,
of becoming old within when still young without.

Help the workers in the industrial countries.
They are enjoying what their predecessors won
in the course of labor struggles.
They should not now turn "middle-class."
They should not forget their brothers and sisters
who are not allowed to unionize;
or those we call foreign workers or guest workers;
or their fellows in the Third World
who cannot even become workers in the full sense
but must remain only proletarians.

May every worker
win a more just and human position
without falling victim to selfishness!

Lord, you know well
that today there are not only
rich and poor individuals.
There are rich, even excessively rich, countries
and there are poor countries.
You know, too, that the difference
is becoming ever greater rather than less.
Help men and women of good will—
from every land and color and language and religion—
to bring liberating moral pressure to bear
on authorities
and awaken their consciences
so that they will help the human race
to be freed from the shame of the subhuman beings
whom wretchedness produces,
and from the shame of the superhuman
who are begotten of excessive prosperity and luxury.

Help those who have the happiness
of being born in rich countries;
help them to see
that the privileges they enjoy
have been bought by injustice
to the poor countries.
Without realizing it,
they often become accomplices
of this injustice.

Have you noticed, Lord,
how in developed and poor countries alike
there are more and more minorities
who, like Abraham,
hope against all hope?
They are determined to build
a more human and more just world.
It is consoling to see them
undertaking peaceful yet bold actions
that will increasingly undermine
oppressive structures.

Lord, you may think the ending of this prayer
somewhat naive—
There is but one richness:
participation in your life, your divinity,
your creative power, your will.
Other riches are false riches,
piled up in selfishness.

Money, power, fame, middle-class complacency
breed selfishness.
Selfishness is the beast that lurks within us,
swallows us up
and leads us to swallow others up.

Help your human creatures
to flee false riches
and plunge into the riches
for which all of us were born:
the one undivided love,
love of God and love of humankind.